Original title:
Meadow Memoirs

Copyright © 2025 Creative Arts Management OÜ
All rights reserved.

Author: Vivian Laurent
ISBN HARDBACK: 978-1-80566-762-9
ISBN PAPERBACK: 978-1-80566-832-9

Tales of Twilight Blossoms

In the garden, a gnome took a dive,
He landed in a pot, oh so alive!
The flowers giggled, petals all aglow,
As he yelled, "Water me! I'm quite the show!"

The bees wore shades, buzzing with flair,
While ants marched by in a funky pair.
They boogied on daisies, spun in delight,
Creating a ruckus from morning to night.

Beneath a Canopy of Stars

The stars twinkled brightly, like fairy lights,
While crickets held concerts on magical nights.
A raccoon in a tux tried to steal the scene,
With a top hat and cane, he was quite the dream!

A firefly dance led to a wild parade,
As owls joined in, wearing capes they made.
Together they laughed, beneath the moon's grin,
In a world full of mischief, where fun would begin.

The Horizon's Gentle Caress

The sun woke up with a stretch and a yawn,
As squirrels held a race, cheering from dawn.
With nuts in their paws, they zoomed through the trees,
While birds played soccer with leaves in the breeze.

The daisies played poker, with caterpillars as peers,
Laughing and joking, despite their small fears.
A butterfly referee waved his tiny flag,
And giggles erupted when the ladybugs bragged.

Time's Gentle Tug

The clock on the wall had a mind of its own,
Tick-tocking and dancing, never alone.
It invited the mice for a dance on the floor,
Who twirled and they spun, crying out for more!

And though time was slippery, like soup on a spoon,
They raced with their hopes 'neath the light of the moon.
The garden was bustling with laughter and cheer,
In this jolly old place, where time disappears!

Silence of the Seedlings

In a quiet patch, they sit and stare,
Little green sprouts without a care.
They whisper secrets to the bright sky,
Dreaming of leaves that will soon fly.

One sprout giggles, 'I'll grow quite tall!'
While another sighs, 'I won't grow at all.'
Together they chat about the rain,
Hoping to dodge a pesky train.

Portraits of a Perfect Day

Butterflies flit in a dizzy dance,
Sipping nectar, a sweet romance.
A squirrel in shades strikes a pose,
While bees buzz tune that nobody knows.

The daisies gossip with a sway,
'What a fine outfit you wore today!'
Sunshine smirks, painting the scene,
Laughter spills where the grass is green.

The Song of the Meadowlark

A meadowlark sings, with a puff and a cheer,
Chasing away all thoughts of fear.
Its notes are silly, a melody free,
Echoing joy under each leafy tree.

It struts with flair, as if in a show,
Each hop a step from head to toe.
Grasshoppers judge, with a twitching brow,
'Can you sing with style? Let me show you how!'

Journeys Through the Wild Grass

In tangled blades, they set off with glee,
A band of ants on their grand spree.
One claims, 'I found a crumb divine!'
The others cheer, 'Now that's a sign!'

They march in line, all full of cheer,
Imagining feasts that soon will appear.
But wait! A raindrop plops on their path,
Sudden chaos and giggles bring forth a laugh!

Solace in the Stillness

In the grass where daisies dance,
I tripped and took a silly chance.
A butterfly stole my lunch away,
I laughed so hard, I couldn't sway.

Bob the squirrel eyed my snack,
He plotted hard, a little hack.
My sandwich now a target bold,
As tales of food are quickly told.

The bees all buzzed their melody,
Like tiny musicians, wild and free.
I tried to join but lost the beat,
And ended up in something sweet.

A rabbit with a fluffy coat,
Observed my dance and then did gloat.
With a wink and nod, he hopped away,
While I got stuck—oh what a day!

Petals Upon the Wind

Tiny petals dance and swirl,
A butterfly does a silly twirl.
Bee in a rush, stings on the fly,
Laughter echoes, how time does fly.

A ladybug slides down a stem,
Scarlet spots, oh what a gem!
Grass tickles toes, a funny fate,
Watch your step, or it's grass, you'll hate!

The Embrace of a Summer's Day

Sunshine beams, the heat is grand,
A squirrel near steals my sandwich hand.
Picnic ants march in perfect line,
I set one free – he claims it's mine!

Clouds drift by in a fluffy rush,
I chase them down, but they just hush.
Ice cream melts, a colorful slap,
My shirt now wears a rainbow cap!

Twilight's Canvas of Colors

Stars peek out with a wink and grin,
Fireflies shine, where do I begin?
I stumble on grass, my dignity's lost,
But glow-worms guide me, no matter the cost!

The moon chuckles from high above,
Whispers secrets of insects in love.
A crickets' choir begins to play,
Oh what a ruckus at close of day!

The Heartbeat of the Hill

Rolling down, oh what a thrill,
Grass stains and giggles, heartbeats spill.
A tumbleweed tickles my nose with glee,
Rolling away, 'Oh please, come back to me!'

Poppies wink as I pass them by,
I tip my hat, they wave goodbye.
Chasing shadows until they flee,
Life's silly dance, just so carefree!

Whispers of the Wildflowers

In a patch of wild, bright cheer,
Daisies giggle, oh so near.
Butterflies dance, no care or woes,
While ants debate, in awkward prose.

A bumblebee's drone sings off-key,
Sipping nectar, oh so free.
Sunshine tickles the grass with glee,
Even worms would join the spree.

Old oak throws shade, a wise ol' chap,
Telling stories, taking a nap.
Squirrels steal nuts with playful grins,
While meadows hum, where fun begins.

Chasing clouds at their own pace,
Laughter echoes, no saving grace.
Underneath the sky so blue,
Nature's folly, a happy crew.

Echoes in the Grassy Expanse

In fields of green, where grasses sway,
Frogs croak jokes, come out to play.
A rabbit hops, in search of snacks,
While crickets plan their dance routines, no lacks.

A wandering breeze comes to tease,
Whispers secrets with every squeeze.
The sun winks down, a cheeky chap,
As daisies shimmy in a floral clap.

A lost shoe makes a game of chase,
Grass stains earned in a clumsy race.
Wind tells tales of the silly sparrow,
Who thought the sky was a giant harrow.

With sunblock on, ants march in line,
Each one thinking today is divine.
In this world where giggles soar,
Nature's antics, forever to explore.

Sunlit Secrets of the Field

Under sunlit skies, a glow,
A ladybug's game is to steal the show.
With a tiny wink, she claims the ground,
While squirrels argue over acorns found.

Dandelions puff, in a silly dance,
Blowing wishes with a quirky glance.
The grass tickles toes that wiggle abound,
As hedgehogs tumble round and round.

A chicken struts, proud as can be,
Clucking tales of glory and glee.
She claims the throne, a regal feat,
While rabbits munch on her discarded treat.

When shadows grow long and day is high,
Even fireflies begin to shy.
With flashes bright, they start to weave,
A tapestry of laughter, 'tis hard to believe.

Tread of Time on Clovers

In a patch of clover, green and bright,
A snail takes its time, to its delight.
Counting each step on slippery ground,
Wonders how many friends can be found.

Grasshoppers leap with boisterous glee,
Challenging clouds for a bit of spree.
While daisies giggle, waving their heads,
And sleepy sheep dream of buttery breads.

Ants in a line navigate their task,
A tiny parade, no questions asked.
As shadows stretch and the day grows dim,
The world laughs on, with a playful whim.

Sunset paints in hues of mad,
Making even the sternest critters glad.
In tales told by fluttering leaves,
Time plays tricks, but fun never leaves.

Remnants of a Rainy Afternoon

Puddles gather all around,
A duck parade, not making a sound.
With splashes here and splashes there,
I chased the splatter, unaware!

Umbrellas up, a game of hide,
I trip, I slip, oh what a ride!
The raindrops laugh, the grass takes dance,
I spin and twirl in a soggy trance.

My socks are soggy, but who would care?
I bubble with laughter, splashing in air.
The sun peeks out, just to tease,
While I look like I've caught the breeze!

Through muddy paths, we make our way,
The world's a mess but bright as day.
With friends beside, the laughter flows,
In rainy revelry, joy only grows.

Flickers of Sunlight in the Thicket

Sunbeams dance upon my nose,
A squirrel chuckles as it goes.
With acorns tossed like little balls,
I laugh as each one softly falls.

The bushes rustle, a game of peek,
A rabbit hops with a funny squeak.
I stand still, pretending to freeze,
While nearby bees buzz with such ease.

But here comes trouble, I hear a shout,
A sneaky fox who's up to scout.
With my sandwich in paw, I take flight,
As he spins around, what a silly sight!

Chasing sunbeams in a joyful race,
I stumble and fumble, falling on my face.
With laughter echoing through the trees,
I find it's bliss beneath the leaves.

Time Stopped Beneath the Oak

Beneath the oak, I lounge with ease,
Watching clouds like drifting cheese.
A ladybug lands on my knee,
We share lunch, just her and me.

The breeze whispers, 'Time to play,'
While ants line up in a parade.
I join them, marching in a line,
Though they don't want me, that's just fine!

A bird above sings quite the tune,
I dance along, a summoned boon.
With twirls and spins, I give a proud bow,
The oak just chuckles, "Oh dear, wow!"

Time stands still in this silly play,
Where laughter blooms in bright array.
With nature's joy, I feel no strain,
Just giggles and grins from sun and rain.

A Patchwork of Petals

Petals flutter, a colorful swirl,
I catch them all, giving a twirl.
A daisy lands upon my hat,
I strut around, feeling quite sprat!

Butterflies dance like ribboned dreams,
While bees hum tunes of sunshine beams.
With pockets full of flowery finds,
I craft a crown for all my friends.

But then, alas, disaster strikes,
A wind gust blows, oh how it hikes!
My flowery crown goes soaring high,
I watch it drift, with a silly sigh.

Yet laughter fills the fragrant air,
As we chase petals without a care.
In nature's quilt, our spirits rise,
Finding joy where the wildflower lies.

Scented Memories of Lavender

In the garden, bees do dance,
Wearing stripes, they take their chance.
Flowers giggle in the breeze,
Tickling noses, such a tease!

Socks are lost amidst the blooms,
Rabbits plotting in their rooms.
Lavender smells like dreams gone wild,
Nature's perfume, so beguiled.

Ants march by with tiny flair,
Carrying crumbs without a care.
A sneaky snail gives a wink,
'Life's too short, come sit and think!'

Hats askew, the gnomes ignite,
Riddles whisper through the night.
Each moment here, so absurd,
Laughter caught in every word.

A Symphony of Crickets' Song

Crickets chirp in perfect tune,
While frogs hop, arm in arm, like a cartoon.
Under stars they sing and sway,
Mocking humans, it's their play.

Grasshoppers jump with wide-eyed glee,
Belly laughs echo—oh, it's free!
Fireflies join in, lights aglow,
A wild dance-off beneath the show.

Mice throw parties, but hush, don't squeak,
They might invite the owl to peek!
Nature's twirls, a comedy act,
Every creature has a knack.

And in this laughter, we'll find delight,
Through every bump and croaky night.
So grab a seat, pull in your ears,
Join the fun, forget your fears!

Where the Sun Meets the Horizon

Chasing shadows, kids run wild,
Kites fly high, oh blissful child!
Sunset paints the sky so bright,
Wibbly wobbly, such a sight.

A dog slips into the mud,
Rolling, tumbling with a thud.
As laughter spills like soda pop,
Watch it drip, don't let it stop!

Squirrels bicker, tails in a knot,
'That acorn's mine!' Oh, is it not?
Twilight giggles, to the trees it whirls,
Whispering secrets to the swirls.

Chasing fireflies, kids yell, 'Whoosh!'
They dance in air, a glowing swoosh.
With each dusk, new tales will rise,
In sunset's glow, we find our prize.

Harvest of Quiet Moments

In the still, the soft winds sigh,
Whispers linger as time drifts by.
Underneath an old oak tree,
Squirrels play hide and seek with glee.

Dusty shoes, a path well-trod,
Mice hold court, pretending to nod.
Kite strings tangle in the breeze,
A riddle shared among the leaves.

Hats on heads, wonky and bright,
Twirling dandelions take flight.
Chasing giggles, we might just find,
Laughter blooming as we unwind.

With every sunset, we collect,
Memories that in joy reflect.
In quiet moments, joy is sown,
In playful hearts, we're never alone.

Mosaic of Memories

In the field where daisies sway,
I tripped on air, hip-hip-hooray!
Butterflies giggled, took to flight,
While I fell down, what a sight!

The sun was bright, my hat was loose,
It flew away, a silly goose!
Chasing shadows, chasing dreams,
I stumbled over my own schemes.

Kites sailed high, or so I thought,
But mine was tangled, oh, woe begot!
Laughter echoed, friends all around,
As I wrestled with the ground.

A picnic feast of crumbs and cheer,
I lost my sandwich—oh dear, oh dear!
Instead of laughter, a bird took flight,
Eating my lunch, what a funny sight!

Cameos of the Creek

By the creek where ripples dance,
I saw a frog in a silly trance.
He croaked a song, oh what a tune,
I joined in, under the afternoon moon.

A dragonfly with a monocle,
Buzzed by me, looking quite comical.
Searching for wisdom in a floral book,
But all he found was a fishy look!

Turtles in hats, what a wild view,
Posing like models, they knew what to do.
A race ensued, they slowly crept,
While I laughed so hard, I almost wept.

Splashing water, I joined the spree,
Only to find my shoe on a tree!
Nature's pranks, forever they stay,
By the creek, where we laugh and play.

Shadows in the Tall Grass

Tall grass whispers of secrets kept,
I lost my friend; he surely wept.
In the shadows, we played hide and seek,
But my giggles gave away my peak.

A rabbit passed, wearing a frown,
It seemed my laughter was bringing him down.
I offered him carrots, sweet and bright,
He jumped away, a comical sight!

The daisies danced without a care,
While we tumbled, feet in the air.
My hat flew off, a gusty surprise,
And landed right on a cow's big eyes!

Those shadows deep where mischief thrives,
We'd laugh so much, we felt alive.
In this tall grass, let joy amass,
Our funny moments, like breezes, pass.

Nature's Serenity Unveiled

In a field of flowers, I sat with glee,
A bee mistook me for a flower, whee!
He buzzed around, quite lost in bliss,
I swatted him down with an awkward swish.

Clouds were fluff, like cotton candy,
Until one dripped rain, oh so dandy!
My friends and I danced in the shower,
Singing songs of the wildflower power.

A squirrel chuckled from a nearby tree,
As I chased my hat, what a sight to see!
Rolling and tumbling, full of cheer,
In Nature's arms, we felt no fear.

With laughter loud and spirits bright,
We captured joy in every light.
These moments passed like summer's breeze,
Funny and sweet, like honeyed teas.

Paintbrushes of the Seasons

Spring splashes green with glee,
While summer throws a wild spree.
Autumn spills orange and gold,
Winter wraps it all, so bold.

A flower sneezes, oh so loud,
The sun shines brightly, feeling proud.
A squirrel dons its winter coat,
And sings a song, a furry note.

Bees dance like they own the town,
While butterflies float, never frown.
Each season paints with colors wide,
In this canvas where laughs abide.

The Flicker of Fireflies at Night

Fireflies blink like disco lights,
As crickets serenade the nights.
A glowworm joins the little show,
Swinging its lanterns to and fro.

The frogs croak tunes that seem quite rare,
While owls hoot gossip from their lair.
A raccoon claps, quite out of tune,
As stars peek in to join the boon.

With winks and twirls, the night spins on,
While moonbeams play tag until dawn.
Each flicker giggles in delight,
In the glow of mischief, oh what a sight.

Tapestry of Trampled Trails

Footprints scatter, left and right,
A trail of chaos, pure delight.
A mud pie here, a stickman there,
A treasure map in fresh warm air.

A rabbit hops and takes a bow,
With every leap proclaiming, 'Wow!'
A bear rolls by to join the fun,
While nerdy deer list all they've won.

Socks get soaked in puddles wide,
Splashes paint our silly ride.
Each path tells tales of laughter bold,
In stories shared, never old.

Celestial Stories in the Breeze

The wind whispers secrets to the trees,
While leaves giggle, swaying with ease.
Clouds wear crowns, in silly arrays,
Telling tales of their cloudy days.

A kite tangles in a chicken's cluck,
As children chase it—oh what luck!
Sunbeams tease the daisies' heads,
While playful shadows dance on beds.

The breeze tickles all it can find,
Spinning yarns, so unconfined.
Each day is a page, fluttering free,
In the book of nature's jubilee.

Echoes of the Breezes

In the field where cows like to chill,
Breezes whisper, oh what a thrill!
A chicken roams, proud and spry,
Clucking tunes to the cotton candy sky.

Grasshoppers hop to a lively beat,
Worms wiggle under foot, quite the treat!
A squirrel steals snacks from a nearby tree,
While butterflies laugh, 'Come dance with me!'

Bees buzz by with a cheeky grin,
Daring the ants to join in the din.
Nature's circus, a strange parade,
Full of giggles that never fade.

When the sun dips low and the stars appear,
The fireflies glow, the laughter is near.
A wind chime sings with bells of glee,
Echoes of joy float so carefree.

A Symphony of Blossoms

Petals are fluttering like a wild dance,
Bees in tuxedos, they take their chance.
A rose giggles as she trips on her stem,
Tulips whisper, 'We'll show them who's glam!'

Daisies declare they're the party's best,
With daffodils nodding, they suit up in zest.
A sunbeam winks, a jester in light,
As blooms chatter away, what a lively sight!

A butterfly steals nectar, oh what a tease,
While ladybugs laugh in the buzzing breeze.
With a dandelion crown, they dance and sway,
In a floral funfair, come join the play!

When twilight comes, dreams start to twirl,
In this colorful chaos, watch laughter unfurl.
Each blossom a note in nature's own song,
Reminding us all that we too can belong.

Secrets Beneath the Ferns

Beneath the fronds where the shaded ones dwell,
Frogs tell jokes, their cackles swell.
A lizard slips by in his snazzy attire,
Chasing his tail like he's stuck in a mire.

A snail with a top hat moves mighty slow,
Claims he may win the great garden show.
But slugs slide in, all crafty and sly,
Together they chuckle, oh my, oh my!

The roots whisper tales to the stones nearby,
While curious mushrooms peek with a sigh.
They giggle about who's the tallest in sight,
As shadows dance on this moonlit night.

When morning breaks, they scatter with pride,
Leaving behind secrets where laughter can hide.
In this sunlit forest where stories are spun,
Every little creature knows how to have fun.

Dances in the Daisies

In a circle of daisies, the critters ignite,
Squirrels get ready, it's party tonight!
With acorns and berries stacked high on a seat,
They munch and they chatter, not missing a beat.

A hedgehog steps up, wearing spiky shoes,
Claims he can dance without missing a groove!
The rabbits all giggle, they twirl and they leap,
As frogs croak a tune that makes everyone peep.

Butterflies twirl in their bright fashion shows,
While bees hum along in their buzz-worthy flows.
The sun casts a spotlight, oh what a display,
In the laughter of blooms, they all join the fray!

As sunset descends on this fanciful scene,
The animals bow, feeling quite like a queen.
In the cheerful patch where the grass feels like fluff,
Each knows that a giggle is always enough!

Rustic Reveries of the Earth

In fields so wide, my hat flew high,
A squirrel laughed as it zipped by.
The cows eyed me with silent glee,
  As if they knew my fate to be.

A frog in boots danced on a log,
While I fell down, just like a dog.
The flowers swayed and giggled too,
As if they shared my clumsy view.

The bees all buzzed, they knew my name,
  Perhaps they thought it was a game.
  With pollen stuck upon my face,
  I joined their dance, a silly chase.

The skies above began to pout,
As rain dropped down, I twisted about.
I splashed in puddles like a kid,
  And laughed until I lost my lid.

Unraveled Threads of Nature

The yarn I tossed to weave my tale,
Got tangled up, it seemed to sail.
The rabbits cheered as it took flight,
While me, I wrestled with delight.

A butterfly stole my lunch today,
With a wink, it fluttered away.
I chased it down, but tripped on grass,
And let out quite the silly gasp.

The hedgehogs hosting a tea event,
Shared stories of where their spines were bent.
With cups of dew and crumpets rare,
I laughed so hard, I dropped my chair.

Then came the ants with hats so grand,
Declaring me their dancing band.
We twirled and swayed until they fled,
They said my moves could wake the dead!

Beneath the Watchful Oak

Underneath a mighty tree,
I lost my shoe, oh woe is me!
The acorns chuckled from above,
As squirrels darted like they loved.

The shadows played a game of catch,
With sunlight creeping, half a match.
A rabbit popped and gave a wink,
Before he bounced off—what to think?

An old raccoon with wisdom deep,
Said, "Nature's full of laughs, not sheep!"
I pondered that—it made me grin,
Was he the sage of all things spin?

With doodles drawn in dirt with glee,
I made a picture, just for me.
But rain came down, a sudden blip,
And my art washed away—what a trip!

The Language of Tall Grass

The tall grass whispered secrets low,
Of crickets' plans and winds that blow.
A bug in specs, reading a map,
Tried to lead me, but fell in a trap.

The daisies giggled at my plight,
As I danced around, trying to fight.
Then came the breeze, it pulled my hair,
And off I spun like I didn't care.

The thistles threw a garden show,
With prickly acts, they stole the glow.
I cheered them on, my sides did ache,
As bees buzzed in—what a funny shake!

The grass revealed a path of glee,
Leading back home, just me—oh me!
I took a bow to nature's jest,
And left the field with a heart at rest.

Beneath the Canopy of Sky

Beneath the sky so wide and blue,
I lost my shoe, oh what a clue!
Bunnies laughing as they hop,
They think my fashion choices flop.

A squirrel danced, a fluffy tail,
I swear it sang a funny tale.
My picnic spread, a sight to see,
But ants declared their victory.

The clouds above, they start to shift,
One looks like cheese, oh what a gift!
A breeze that tickles, makes me squeal,
The joy this day is quite surreal.

With giggles echoing round the glade,
I can't believe the games we've played.
As shadows stretch and sunlight fades,
I'll chase a butterfly that parades.

Lullabies of the Land

In the fields where daisies bloom,
A goat named Fred, who thinks he's cool.
With tiny socks upon his feet,
He struts around, a farmyard feat.

Frisky lambs begin to play,
They jump around in such a sway.
A lullaby of laughter stays,
For all to hear on sunny days.

There's Mike the pig, he loves to roll,
In mud so thick, he feels quite whole.
The chorus of the crows above,
Sing silly tunes, it's purest love.

As dusk descends, the fireflies glow,
A jolly dance, they put on a show.
We laugh and dream, till night does blend,
With all these tales, the fun won't end.

A Dance of Dandelions

Dandelions sway in gentle cheer,
Spinning round, they'll disappear.
With a gust, they take to flight,
A golden whirl, what a delight.

A couple of ants on a tiny quest,
Climbing high, they're doing their best.
They march like soldiers, hats askew,
Dancing with pollen, all brand new.

Butterflies flutter, oh what a sight,
They bump into clouds, they hide from light.
With every breeze, a chuckle shared,
Each leap they take, someone's ensnared.

When dusk arrives, the crickets cheer,
The dandelion dreams bring us near.
These silly moments, filled with jest,
Oh, how they fill our hearts with zest!

Pastoral Reflections at Dusk

As the sun dips low, shades fade away,
A frog sings loudly, he's gone astray.
He croaks his dreams to all who hear,
While sheep roll eyes, they know no fear.

In fields of grass, we play and roam,
An unexpected goat strolls home.
He looks so proud with a sprig of thyme,
His antics always steal the rhyme.

The twilight laughs, it knows our plight,
We trip on roots, in fading light.
And as the day bids us farewell,
Stories unfold, we giggle and dwell.

So here we pause, the fun we share,
In every moment, laughter's flair.
As stars emerge in darkened skies,
We hold dear these wacky ties.

The Language of Petals

The flowers whisper secrets on a breeze,
They giggle and shimmy, like clumsy bees.
Roses gossip, daisies plot,
Tulips boast, while lilies are caught.

A daisy asked, 'What's with the frown?'
'I've lost my hat,' said a sunflower down.
They laugh and twirl in a wild charade,
As tulip friends throw a colorful parade.

Then comes the wind, in a playful swirl,
Knocking petals down for a dizzying twirl.
They sing in chorus, what a loud tune!
Pollen's packed up, who will see the moon?

The dance floor's set with a carpet of green,
Floral ballet, what a silly scene.
So come join in, don't be shy,
Let's gossip with flowers and reach for the sky!

Serendipity Among Stalks

In a field of tall grass, quite the surprise,
A rabbit danced, with googly eyes.
Chasing a butterfly, round and round,
They tripped and fell on soft, bouncy ground.

A buzzard squawked, 'What is this ruckus?'
While a frog croaked, 'Can I join your circus?'
Laughter erupted from blooms all around,
As mischief spread on the soft ground.

A scarecrow chuckled, 'I've lost my hat!'
As bees gathered, no time to chat.
With petals aflutter, the laughter just soared,
In the perfect place where silliness poured.

Wind chimes rang, with a jolly clang,
As daisies belted out a funny tang.
Together they danced, free and light,
In this whimsical world, everything felt right.

Footprints in the Clover

Stumbling through clovers, shoes all a mess,
My foot found a worm, oh, what a stress!
It wriggled and giggled, 'What's all the fuss?'
I apologized, oh dear, what a blundering plus!

Out bounced a squirrel, with a nut in tow,
'What did you do, make a mud show?'
With acorns a-fling, he joined in the game,
While I blushed, it's all quite the same.

A ladybug flew by, a royal decree,
'Let's have some fun, come play with me!'
We frolicked and tumbled in the green sea,
While a bumblebee buzzed, declaring, 'Yippee!'

With laughter echoing, what a delightful chase,
In this frolicsome land, there's no wrong place.
So leave tracks in clover, with joy on your face,
And hop like a bunny in this silly race!

Scented Memories of Summer

The scent of blooms brought old tales to mind,
Of mishaps and laughter, oh how we've dined!
A garden party turned into a race,
When ants marched in, taking over the place.

We threw crumb cakes, to shoo them away,
But they cha-cha'd closer, in a brave ballet.
I giggled at chaos, oh what a sight,
While a gopher peeked out, eager for a bite.

A sunbeam winked, as clouds played peek,
While daisies debated, 'Who is the meek?'
Between teasing and laughter, time took its toll,
But silly blooms always make the heart whole.

As summer fades, and fall waves goodbye,
Memories linger, like stars in the sky.
So cherish those moments, let joy always bloom,
In your heart's lush garden, it'll always have room!

The Rustle of Forgotten Days

In the grass, I found a shoe,
A relic of a time I knew.
It squeaked and chirped beneath my foot,
I laughed so hard, I lost my loot.

A picnic set with ants galore,
They danced around, what was in store?
An old sandwich, green and spry,
I tossed it high, oh me, oh my!

The trees whispered tales of yore,
Each leaf a secret, legend, lore.
I listened close, they chuckled loud,
As I tripped over a sleeping cloud.

A squirrel scolded me for fun,
Claimed I was in his way to run.
I bowed my head, I did retreat,
The critter laughed, a small defeat.

Rain Kisses on Earth

Raindrops plinked like tiny drums,
Announcing all the clumsy chums.
Umbrellas flipped, a cinematic show,
Splashing puddles, yelling, 'Go! Go!'

A snail slid by without a care,
Wearing rain like a fancy pair.
I tried to share my candy stash,
He looked at me and tried to dash.

Raindrops danced like laughter sprung,
With every drop, a joke was sung.
I twirled around, my hair a mess,
The clouds grinned down, I must confess.

A frog proclaimed it was his day,
And jumped on my head in playful play.
We leapt and hopped, what a fine sight,
Until the sun said, 'You're too bright!'

Sundown's Golden Embrace

As daylight fades, the sky's a show,
With orange and pink, a perfect glow.
I waved goodbye to the sun's grand act,
And tripped over shadows, oh, what a fact!

The crickets chirped a funky beat,
I danced along, my two left feet.
A firefly thought I was a star,
It flickered close, then zoomed afar.

The twilight air was filled with cheer,
As I told jokes to a passing deer.
It laughed so hard, I lost my breath,
And ran away, dodging certain death!

The moon peeked out, a cheeky grin,
Whispering tales of where I'd been.
I yawned and wished upon that light,
Wondering if the stars get fright!

A Canvas of Colors

In fields of blooms, I found my paint,
With colors bold, not shy, nor quaint.
I dipped my toes in daisies bright,
   A mix of chaos, pure delight.

Bees buzzed tales of their grand flights,
While butterflies flaunted their new tights.
I tried to catch one for my hat,
   But it giggled, and just sat.

A dog rolled in some blue forget-me-nots,
It emerged looking like it fought with pots.
We shared a laugh, a puffy plume,
And painted the air with scents that bloom.

As day turned to night, I sighed with pride,
My masterpiece, no need to hide.
In nature's gallery, I found my muse,
On this canvas of colors, I chose to cruise.

Harvesting Sunlit Days

In fields of gold, we danced and played,
With butterflies, our lively brigade.
We chased the sun, with squeals of glee,
While ants debated their grand history.

A picnic set, a sandwich split,
The turf our stage, where laughter lit.
With ants in line, and bees in flight,
We marked the day a pure delight.

In sun-kissed hours, our antics soared,
Like ketchup on fries that can't be ignored.
We'd race the wind, then trip over roots,
Our giggles echoing like playful hoots.

As day bids farewell with colors bright,
We'll recount our tales 'neath the soft twilight.
With one last laugh, we pack our stay,
In sunny fields, we'll find our way.

A Ballet of Swaying Grass

The grass stood tall, a curtain call,
As breezes brushed, just like a ball.
With bugs in tuxes, they swayed and pranced,
If only humans could join their dance!

A ladybug leads; oh so refined,
While crickets chirp, in rhythm aligned.
We watched in awe, these fellows brave,
Each twirl and dip, the chaos they crave.

But oops! A gust, and down it goes,
A rogue tumbleweed steals the show!
The audience chuckles, and in delight,
We clap along 'til the fall of night.

So here we sit with snacks in tow,
As nature performs a comical show.
In grassy halls, where laughter spills,
We cheer for the troupe with wild thrills!

Curiosities of the Leafy Glade

In thickets deep, where whispers dwell,
A squirrel told tales, and we knew them well.
Of acorns stashed for the winter's bite,
And secret talks 'neath the moon's soft light.

The mushrooms grinned, with colors bright,
Said, 'Join our party! It's quite a sight!'
But hesitance reigned; were they confetti?
We laughed and left, still feeling petty.

A frog in a crown, practicing croaks,
Announced his reign with a series of jokes.
His royal decree? No rain on parade—
Unless he slips and lands in the shade!

This leafy glade, a wild menagerie,
Where nature's fun lives in its own treasury.
We skedaddle back, our hearts so light,
To share the wonders of the delightful night.

The Embrace of Earth and Sky

Beneath the vault of the laughing sky,
We launched paper planes that dared to fly.
With every toss, a hopeful sigh,
Would they soar high or just say goodbye?

Clouds sat giggling, as each plane crashed,
In the muddy sea, our dreams were dashed.
But from the ground, we made a plan,
With cardboard wings, we'd take a stand!

The daisies cheered, our biggest fans,
As we concocted flight-ambitious plans.
For who needs wings when you have style?
We strutted proudly, hearts full of guile.

From earth to sky, such mischief brewed,
In nature's arms, we felt renewed.
A cycle of giggles and tangled hair,
In flights of fancy, we banished despair.

The Cricket's Evening Song

A cricket sings with all his might,
His serenade beneath the night.
With little jumps, he claims his stage,
Just a tiny bug, but full of rage.

The moonlit grass, his audience wide,
As fireflies dance, they can't decide.
Should they light up or join the tune?
They flicker 'round like a cartooned moon!

Then comes the snail, slow and aloof,
He slips and slides and goes 'woof woof?'
With such odd sounds, they start to laugh,
A mischievous troop—a merry half!

Then all at once, they join the spree,
Making melodies, wild and free.
For in the night, with glee unfurled,
A cricket's song, the quirkiest world!

Beneath the Canopy of Dreams

Two squirrels plotting with nifty schemes,
Chasing shadows through golden beams.
One stole a nut, oh what a caper,
The other grumbled, 'You little paper!'

A feathered friend chirps with glee,
Poised on a branch, 'Come fly with me!'
But the cat twitches, with an eye for snacks,
While the birds gossip, 'No, we won't relax!'

Dandelions dress like tiny suns,
While ants march by, all in runs.
A picnic planned just for a crowd,
Until the wind cheers and shouts out loud!

The chaos grows, the laughter sings,
As grasshoppers jive and frogs spread wings.
In this realm, hilarities burst,
Who knew nature can really rehearse?

Wanderlust in Bloom

A dandelion dreams of far-off lands,
With wishes as soft as its feathery hands.
It puffs its seeds with such grand delight,
Hoping to travel and take flight.

A bumblebee buzzes, oh what a thrill,
Sipping sweet nectar, but can't sit still.
It trips on the petals, wearing a frown,
And whispers, 'Flowers—let's paint this town!'

Butterflies twirl, with colors so bright,
Matching the giggles of daisies in flight.
They wink at the sun, play tag with the breeze,
While grass blades wave, 'Come join us, please!'

But wait—what's that? A garden hose!
Spraying water like a clown's nose.
Everyone dances, the slip-and-slide scoots,
In this perplexing, fun-filled loot!

Hummingbird Reveries

A hummingbird darts like a speedy thought,
Sipping from flowers, oh what a pot!
It pauses to wink, full of cheeky delight,
'Can you catch me?' it dares, a marvelous flight.

With wings like rainbows, it flits to and fro,
Each stop a burst of loud 'hello!'
The blossoms blush, enchanted and spellbound,
As nectar turns sweet, swirling all around.

But what's that? A bee with a tiny scowl,
'You're hogging the drinks, you little fowl!'
Their tiny squabble tickles the air,
While flowers laugh, "Who needs a care?"

In a swirl of colors, chaos and cheer,
These tiny titans just want a beer!
But flowers know; they need no buzz,
Just a bit of humor, and everything's fuzz!

Musings Under the Ancient Sky

Under the broad and endless dome,
I ponder on how grass is home.
Squirrels plot in their secret glee,
While ants debate who's best at tea.

The clouds drift by with a lazy grace,
They take their time, no rush in their pace.
I wonder if they're just as bizarre,
As folks who claim they can dodge a car.

The sun beams down, a curious peer,
Do flowers laugh when I walk near?
And do they giggle with delight,
When bumblebees give them a fright?

A fox trots by, in a hurry to flee,
Chased by a rabbit who's full of glee.
What a spectacle amidst the green,
Life's a comedy, or so it seems!

A Chorus of Rustling Reeds

In the wind's embrace, the reeds do sway,
They whisper secrets in a silly way.
Like gossipers clad in leafy garbs,
They chuckle at frogs and their floppy jabs.

A crane attempts to dance in the breeze,
But trips on a twig and falls with ease.
The reeds erupt in a riotous cheer,
As poor Mr. Crane turns a shade of sheer.

The ducklings quack a tune out of sync,
While trying to find their way to drink.
Synchronized they are not, at all,
Their haphazard march makes me chortle and brawl.

The sun-tipped reeds bask in the jest,
Life's humor unfolds, it's simply the best.
Each rustle and giggle makes the day bright,
In this whimsical world, everything's right.

Whispers of Wildflowers

Wildflowers whisper with petals so bold,
Telling tales of insects and legends untold.
A colorful bumblebee swings by for a chat,
While daisies gossip, all thanks to the cat.

The daisies say, "Did you see that great feat?
The cat leapt high, but I dodged in retreat!"
The lilies chime in, "Oh do spill the tea,
Last week I inspired a lovely bee spree!"

Sunflowers strut with their heads held high,
"Just what is the secret? Tell me, oh my!"
The answer? A wink and a playful twirl,
As they stretch up to give the sun a whirl.

Every bloom's a comedian in their own right,
With laughter that dances in warm sunlight.
In this patch of cheer, all troubles take flight,
Where wildflowers bloom with pure delight.

Sunlight on the Greens

Sunlight spills like honey on the ground,
Making every tiny bug dance around.
A grasshopper jumps with a theatrical flair,
While I try not to trip on my own care.

The daisies giggle as I stumble about,
They whisper, "Watch out, it's a clumsy route!"
The clovers join in with a chuckle or two,
Making fun of me as I lose my shoe.

But I smile back, for it's all in good fun,
Nature knows how to brighten the run.
A sunbeam tickles the back of my neck,
And I start imagining a dance like a wreck!

With each skip and slide, my worries unwind,
For laughter is free when you're in the wild kind.
Amongst all the greens where silliness flows,
We share in the joy that nature bestows.

The Allure of the Open Field

In the field where rabbits race,
A tortoise wonders, 'What's my place?'
Birds in the trees chirp a silly tune,
As the cow tips its hat to the moon.

Grasshoppers hold their jumping contests,
While a snail brags about its best quests.
The farmer's sheep are plotting a prank,
On the old dog snoozing by the tank.

A crow steals a cap from a goat,
The fields echo laughter, what a gloat!
Under the sun, they all come alive,
In this field, every critter can thrive.

The wind whispers jokes through the leaves,
While the flowers giggle and tease.
This lively place where trouble brews,
Is where nature hides its best news.

Harmony in the Haze

In the morning mist, a rooster shrieks,
While a pig acclaims his muddy streaks.
The fog swirls in a comical dance,
Every creature here takes a chance.

A wise old owl with spectacles thick,
Says, 'Watch the fox, he's up to a trick.'
The rabbits chuckle at his sly grin,
As the donkey joins in, flailing a spin.

Up in the trees, the squirrels conspire,
Over acorns they'll surely retire.
The bees buzz around, sharing sweet lore,
While ants juggle crumbs – who could ask for more?

This haze is a canvas for laughter and fun,
In the morning light, the world's come undone.
With every giggle, the day starts anew,
In the embrace of the thick, dewy blue.

The Dance of the Butterflies

Butterflies twirl in a whimsical flight,
Challenging bees to join in the plight.
A ladybug winks, joins the show,
While a caterpillar says, 'I'll steal the glow!'

Around the blooms, they tease and pirouette,
Each one vying for the title of best bet.
A bumblebee hums a tune off-key,
As the flowers laugh, 'Oh, let it be!'

A gust of wind sends them spinning wide,
A butterfly lands – right on a cow's hide.
Laughter erupts from blossoms so bright,
In this garden world, everything feels right.

As the sun sets low, colors all blaze,
In the humor of nature, hearts quickly raise.
From petal to petal, they tiptoe and glide,
In the grand ballet where no one can hide.

Treasures in the Thickets

In the thickets where secrets abound,
A raccoon rummages, what's he found?
A shiny spoon, a shoe, or a hat,
Each item sparks laughter, imagine that!

The squirrels trade stories of things seen,
While the fox breaks in, acting quite mean.
'That's my treasure!' he yells with a grin,
But the raccoon just giggles, 'Come join in!'

Amongst the brambles, a treasure chest lies,
Full of lost socks and the owl's old ties.
A hedgehog pops in and steals the show,
With a wink and a nod, he's ready to go.

When twilight falls, the thickets explode,
With tales of the treasures and laughter bestowed.
In this hidden nook where joys intertwine,
Nature's funny side is simply divine.

Echoes of the Afterglow

Bouncing bunnies in the grass,
Doing yoga, what a laugh!
A hedgehog on a skateboard flies,
While mushrooms giggle, oh my, oh my!

A squirrel's sunbathe, quite a sight,
Chasing shadows, taking flight.
The daisies chuckle at the ants,
Dancing round like silly plants.

Bees tell jokes about their buzz,
Giggling blooms, it's all a fuzz.
The worms hold contests, who can squirm,
While crickets play the funniest term.

So gather 'round, let merriment grow,
In patches where the laughter flows.
With each step, uncover the fun,
In a world where joy has just begun.

Woven Memories Amongst the Stems

In the patch where daisies flirt,
A sheep wears socks, oh how absurd!
They laugh at cows who try to rhyme,
Mooing verses all the time.

A butterfly's the dance instructor,
Twisting petals like a conductor.
The beetles roll in party hats,
While ladybugs clap, imagine that!

The sun dips low with a warm glow,
While ants debate the best taco.
Silly voices fill the air,
Like whispers in a game of dare.

So come and join this vaudeville show,
Where everything's wacky, don't you know?
Amongst the stems of laughter's gleam,
Life is just one grandiose dream.

Garden of Gossamer Dreams

In a garden where the daisies bloom,
A lizard sings out a funny tune.
With tickling toes, it hops around,
While snails play poker on the ground.

The chipmunks juggle acorns high,
As butterflies love to dive and fly.
Amid the vines, the laughter spills,
Like fizzy drinks, it froths and thrills.

A cat in sunglasses takes a stroll,
Meowing riddles, that's his goal.
And every flower has a view,
Of all the antics that ensue.

Life's a circus, don't you see?
In this patch of whimsy, carefree.
With whispers sweet and giggles bright,
The garden's joy shines, pure delight.

Threads of Light in the Field

A gopher wearing a monocle,
Ponders deeply, oh so comical.
While sunflowers sport their best hats,
And giggle at the fluffy sprats.

In the field, where shadows prance,
Caterpillars hold a dance chance.
They stumble, tumble, to the beat,
With clumsy twirls that can't be beat.

The fog rolls in, but doesn't care,
It joins the fun, a fluffy bear.
Frogs croak jokes in silly voices,
As every critter makes their choices.

So weave your dreams in cheerful threads,
Where laughter echoes, and joy spreads.
In every corner, finds a smile,
Life's a treasure, enjoy the while!

Fragrant Pages of the Past

In the field where daisies play,
A cow thinks it's a cabaret.
With grass skirts flying in the breeze,
She jives with squirrels and buzzing bees.

Old bugs share tales on crooked stems,
Of summer days and wild mayhem.
A ladybug in sunglasses glows,
As ants do pirouettes in rows.

Shimmers of Dew at Dawn

Morning light brings bubbles bright,
Dewdrops dance in sheer delight.
A snail on stilts struts with flair,
Atop a leaf, without a care.

Grasshoppers holding a talent show,
Laugh so loud, it's quite a blow.
While frogs in tuxedos croak and cheer,
Their ministrel tunes are wildly queer.

Whimsical Wanderings

A butterfly with painted wings,
Claims he's here for all the swings.
He calls the ants his tiny team,
That's when the fireflies start to beam.

Chasing shadows, they broke free,
Spilling laughter, oh so glee.
With petals worn like pirate hats,
They sail away on whispers, spats.

The Quietude of Nature's Heart

A rabbit in his finest hat,
Bakes carrot cakes, imagine that!
With berries sweet and sprinkles bright,
He shares a slice, oh what a sight!

The trees all nod in-wise surprise,
As giggles float through sunny skies.
And in the hush, you hear them say,
"Nature's funny, night and day!"

The Grass Speaks Softly

In the field, the blades all sway,
They gossip softly, come what may.
"Watch the bees—aren't they a mess?"
"I know, but they sure do impress!"

Dandelions join in, bright and bold,
"I was here first, or so I'm told!"
While clovers chuckle, feeling spry,
"Don't mind them, they're full of high and dry!"

A snail glides past, taking it slow,
"Why rush, when there's so much to know?"
The grass nods with a twinkling breeze,
"Yeah, let's just watch the world, if you please!"

Chasing shadows, a squirrel darts by,
"Catch me if you can!" with a wink in his eye.
The grass laughs, rustles, mightily so,
"You'd be surprised at what we can know!"

Lost in the Lavender Haze

Clouds of purple, a curious sight,
Bumblebees buzzing, taking flight.
"I lost my way—hey, is that my hat?"
"Nope, it's mine! You can have that chitchat!"

Petals dancing, playing hide and seek,
Lavender whispers, a little cheek.
"I'm not your pillow, don't take a nap!"
"But I'm fluffy! Just take a lap!"

A butterfly flutters, giggling along,
"I'll join in your game, it won't take long!"
With a swirl and a twirl, they leap and glide,
"We're off, don't wait—just come for the ride!"

Even the breeze is chuckling today,
Twirling around, in a playful ballet.
"Can't find my way out? Well, that's alright!"
"Let's just stay lost till the stars shine bright!"

Reflections at Twilight's Edge

As daylight dims, the critters convene,
Chattering away near the shady green.
A frog croaks loudly, a silly old joke,
"What did the fly say? 'You're just a bloke!'"

The fireflies twinkle, as night starts to fall,
"Time for some fun! Let's light up the hall!"
Cicadas chuckle, vibrating with glee,
"Can you hear our song? Come dance with me!"

A raccoon peeks out, with a snack in his paws,
"I'm just here munching, without any laws!"
The others all nod, in agreeably fun,
"At twilight's edge, we can't be outrun!"

With laughter and chatter, the night takes flight,
Every shadow dashing, in sheer delight.
"Let's make new stories, before we're all done!"
"And let's not forget our dance under the moon!"

A Tapestry of Tansy

In the garden of colors, all bright and loud,
Tansy twirls proudly, drawing a crowd.
"I'm the queen here! I'm bold, can't you see?"
"Oh please! Just let me be me, can't you agree?"

Daisies chip in, with a laugh and a spin,
"Join us for tea? Where do we begin?"
The breeze whispers softly, teasing the leaves,
"Let's throw a party, who believes?"

A ladybug zooms, in her polka-dot dress,
"Watch out for me! I'm here to impress!"
"Steady there, dear! It's all in good fun!"
"Just don't take too long, we're not quite done!"

The sun starts to fade, and shadows extend,
"Make a wish quick, on me you depend!"
The laughter of flowers fills up the space,
As bright blooms gather in this joyful place!

Stories Woven in Bloom

In a patch of daisies, dogs play hide,
Bumblebees buzz, they take a ride.
A cow named Bessie tells jokes with glee,
While grass tickles toes, oh so free.

A squirrel's acrobatics, quite a sight,
Stealing snacks, it dances in the light.
The daisies giggle, swaying along,
As butterflies join in, humming a song.

But watch your step, oh dear friend of mine,
For muddy puddles might make you pine.
Splashes erupt, laughter fills the air,
As the flowers sway without a care.

When the sun dips low, tales are spun,
Of silly antics, oh what fun!
In the whispers of petals, secrets bloom,
As night begins to cast its loom.

Dancing Shadows Among the Hay

In golden fields where shadows play,
Rabbits hop, making a ballet.
A scarecrow sings, but can't hold a tune,
While crickets strum on their magical rune.

The farmer trips over his own two feet,
Chasing chickens, oh what a feat!
With every quack and every cluck,
They form a chorus, oh what luck!

The sunset paints the sky bright pink,
As everyone stops just to think.
Why did the cow cross over the lane?
To laugh at the goat during its reign!

As stars twinkle in velvet skies,
A party starts, to our surprise!
With fireflies twinkling in the night,
The field's alive, what a delight!

When Butterflies Remember

A butterfly named Lou took a stroll,
Met a worm who was digging a hole.
"Why dig when you can fly like me?"
The worm just chuckled, "You'll wait and see!"

A pair of ants with tiny hats,
Bickered over crumbs and the best of beds.
"I get the cheese, you take the bread!"
They argued loudly, till a bird said, "Fed?"

Now ladybugs giggle on a leaf,
While spiders weave tales of disbelief.
"What if frogs had wings instead?"
"Then they'd hop around and book a bed!"

As dusk approaches, all creatures unite,
Exchanging jokes in the friendly night.
With laughter ringing through the lush bloom,
They spread joy, lighting up the gloom.

Serene Footprints in the Green

Amidst the blades, a child skips by,
Her laughter echoes, reaching the sky.
With each little jump, a butterfly bends,
Twirling and swirling, oh what fun it sends.

Next to the brook, where ripples play,
A frog wears glasses and croaks, 'Hooray!'
"What's your secret to such great style?"
He smirks and says, "Just hop a while!"

In the daisies, a picnic unfolds,
With ants as guests, breaking the mold.
Cookies are crumbled, treats disappear,
While the ants dance, full of cheer.

As the sun sets, gentle and grand,
Footprints tell stories, easy to stand.
With every giggle, a memory stays,
In the whispers of green, in sunny rays.

www.ingramcontent.com/pod-product-compliance
Lightning Source LLC
Chambersburg PA
CBHW071835160426
43209CB00003B/302